Slow-Moving Target

Slow-Moving Target

Sue Wheeler

Brick Books

CANADIAN CATALOGUING IN PUBLICATION DATA

Wheeler, Sue, 1942–
  Slow-moving target

Poems.
ISBN 1-894078-08-X

1. Title.

PS8595.H3853S56 2000   C811'.54   C00-930592-0
PR9199.3.W43S56 2000

Copyright © Sue Wheeler, 2000.

We acknowledge the support of the Canada Council for the Arts for our publishing programme. The support of the Ontario Arts Council is also gratefully acknowledged.

The cover image of Long Beach, B.C. is by Sue Wheeler. The author photo is by Peter Johnston.

Typeset in Junius. Stock is acid-free Zephyr Antique laid. Printed and bound by the Porcupine's Quill Inc.

Brick Books
431 Boler Road, Box 20081
London, Ontario N6K 4G6

brick.books@sympatico.ca

Table of Contents

I.
A Conversation of Blackbirds 9
The Age of Grasses 10
That Night 11
Last Night 13
Snow Diary 15
Grace 17
Mississippi Eclipse 18
Sediment 20

II.
War Baby 27
Aldredge Place 28
In Juarez 36
Halley, 1986 38
Early Years: Her Kitchen 40
Later Years: Her Mornings 41
Altar 42
Closet Suicide 43
My Father Drops By 45

III.
Not the Whole Story 49
Time Travel 51
Nonsense 52
1970s: Domestic 53
Javelinas 54
Negative Space 56

IV.
Islands   59

V.
A Brief History of Time   69
Field Report   70
Oaxaca: Renoir's 'Luncheon of the Boating Party'   71
Instructions to the Rain   72
December 6th   73
Crossing   74
Chaos, February 2nd   76
Cousins   77
Elegy   78
The Last Bright Morning   79
You Take Me to Your Hometown   80
San Josef Bay   81
Rain Starts and Stops   82
Nomad   83

I

A Conversation of Blackbirds

(for Lynn and Karen)

Fling of ink at sunset, a language
we can't read, syllables swooping

to settle on a trellis-work
of winter stalks and rushes. Women jog

this valley of oak and fennel,
and yesterday a bobcat. The redwings

lift in unison to fold themselves
over the next hedgerow. Down

at the beach, a man casts his hook
and sinker onto the surf. We shout through

the wind *What are you catching?* He lifts
his hands in two karate chops, the one

that got away. Look! The birds
are still at it: forty-as-one? one-as-

forty? Dice without spots, several
dozen *I Chings*. Anything could happen.

The Age of Grasses

(for Selina, 1980–1996)

August morning. Crows and things
   on the tide flat. Trees rewinding
      their shadows as the sun

climbs. Last night we waited
   for meteors and labelled
      constellations. Remember:

half the earth never sees
   these arrangements. Someone
      has convinced us we'll find stars

from the bottom of a well.
   Not so, but Venus,
      when you learn how, can be spotted

in daylight. A child carries
   forgiveness into the world
      the way the osprey tucks her wings

and drops, whether or not the fish
   will keep the appointment.
      A breeze leans on the tawny

grass as it always has
   in this age of grasses,
      of accident and luck.

That Night

If asked about that ancient night
we first made love, we'd each of us say *moon*,
we'd say *dry grasses* and
the long reflection down the bay.

August everywhere, but only
in this one meadow and moment do the grasses
bow to a distant ragtime – wind, the sun's angle –
and the beauty is,
someone glances out at the exact instant
to catch them dancing in place, little pistons of gold
that when the earth turns,
are grass again.

All day you hunt for something –
keys, the name of that author.
If you had a chart, if you had
a beeper for those keys.
And beauty. Where is that on your map?

Memory, too, is an insect that jitters
a little to one side, heads down a dry gulch
or etches a track slightly north of what really took place
so that decades later
two grown-up brothers are laughing and arguing
No it was *you* who cast the bamboo pole and string,
I was the one who got hooked.

Because we'd both be wrong about that night.
The not-yet-dewed-upon grass, the moon
letting down her watered silver ladder
came from several nights before. Framed
our knowing that soon we would step across a line,
astonish ourselves and hurt people.
As we re-drew the map of the world.

Last Night

> *How shall I touch you unless it is everywhere?*
> – Mary Oliver

i. The Fall southeasterly batters
the skylight and I keep waking
to the scent of your skin, a lizard
at the season's turn, craving
the ridge of day-warmed basalt.
An alder cracks and falls and morning
leaks across the new-laid floor.
Later we'll cruise the fenceline
for a breach where deer could step in.

All summer the birds sang *Quick,
three beers!* and *Sweet, sweet-sweet.*
We racketed through slabs of light,
more than two people could ever squander.
Tomorrow I'm gone for weeks, I bitch
about my ticket, the places and times
of arrival, but really it's the old fear
I won't make it back. Over porridge
you whisper *Me too.*

ii. One evening in August we paddled home,
the sky a lilac room, the water
satin around us, quilted
by needles of rain. Lightning
fumed the horizon, each bony finger
announcing the clap and rumble
to follow. All this and still the sun
beckoned low before us, it shook out
a runner of sparked coins.
One of us looked back
and saw the half-rainbow
vaulting the saltchuck.

iii. This storm will finish the garden, dahlias
melted to wads of tissue, relics
of a parade. The wind will have its way
with the Michaelmas daisies.
I'd forgotten how each autumn the heart
sloughs its old skin and fattens,
how it shoves the ribcage like a fetus.
Last night the moon raced
back-lit clouds. So hard
to tell what's moving
from what's moving less.

Snow Diary

1. One Thing About Snow

It's like we're hung over.
Where are we?
Who said those crazy things?
It snows, and the air
is a skein of twisted words.
The third day we manage a longish walk.

One thing about snow,
it testifies who's been there: child
in gumboots, deer, otter, mouse.
                                    When we slip
into loops of resentment
it's too cold or too hot everywhere.
How do the little creatures get by?
We even see a spider letting herself down
on a thread of her own device.
I'll tell you something:
Once, and for a long time, I thought
I was a slow-moving target for love.
Today I'd settle for a truce
with what is fixed and repetitive
in myself. Lines and circles of footprints
plod past the bare-armed cherry.

Where are you?

2. *Otherwise*

It was a fine snow, as snow goes,
and its going summoned all kinds of evidence:
crocus and iris, laundry on the line.
Summoned me eight feet in the air
to clip and saw, helping the apple tree
find green reminders of her best self.
Why do I bank the hurts and careless words?
(Nero, in that 50s epic,
saying 'Septimus, bring me my tear vial.')
Thank god you take stock otherwise:
good times, dependabilities, gifts.
It's all how you count. One,
one, the whiter-than-white buffleheads
slip beneath the water.
Clean-as-they'll-get shirts are pegged
in place, blind as busts of emperors.
Their arms reach. A breezy faith
rises and passes through them.
I am the one who carries tools
up a ladder. Who decides how to shape
this tree.

Grace

Chunk-chunk, the post-hole digger
separates *this* from *that*
along a fenceline.
The sapsucker circles the cherry trunk
and ignores you. Ignores me too,

panning a word for *grace*.
Bird-feeder you call this tree,
robins dropping in from all over the map
the day the cherries darken.
April, the wind lifts a blizzard

off limbs clotted thick as the tissue
flowers I pleated over bobby pins
in Miss Winter's class. Did we imagine
carnations would bank the halls
of our lives? *I sell dreams*

the nurseryman said
as we freed the bare stick
from his sawdust. O's of amazement
necklace the bark, and the bird
keeps drilling.

Mississippi Eclipse

Drink me! the straight-up moon
tells the river, plate
yourself in silver scales,
as the track snakes alongside
and singles lurch to the bar car
to name their poison. Some say the death
of nature's upon us,
everything Disneyfied
and shrink-wrapped in package
tours. Moon lost her virginity
with one small step
but she's still got this trick
up her sleeve.
         Oh,
we've copped to alignment,
that cosmic chiropractor,
and how a body
hauls its double through light.
No trackside peasant will fall
to his knees tonight, or villages
craze with believers. We flash
past the squares of cold blue
light they doze in front of,
one arm slack on the broadloom
like an old idea. Einstein's
Observer in Space watched a spinning
planet, a train, a fly
buzzing the insomniac club car:
what moves?

The wolf's at the door, as usual,
and nobody here but us
billions, caught between sun
and moon, throwing the one
round shadow. Which brings us to bypass
the *NO!* in the vestibule
and unlatch the glass,
angling our necks, lunatic herons
whispering *relative*
as the whole kit and caboose
goes *double-S double-S I,*
all the way to Chicago.

Sediment

> *we came from the culture of fishes beforehand*
> *the teeming at certain rocks excites us truly*
> *thought is sediment, laid down, beautiful*
> — Erin Mouré

The stories begin *So this* guy *goes into this* bar.
The other one figure-eights her cloth over the varnish

and doesn't catch his name. Glasses hang like newborns,
like carp in a topsyturvy pool, *Australia* some joker's bound to crack.

Two in a room, swapping molecules through the breathed air.
Who do we think we are?

* * *

Some show up giftwrapped for the Have caste, little name tags,
Hi! I'm (Your Name). I get food and medicine!

I walk out into the Christmas sunrise,
full moon setting pink behind pink mountains.

On the news: people this morning head back to dangerous homelands.
Wish list for the mother on the forced march: *Bread. A new lullaby.*

A cracked privilege, presuming anyone's heart
from the cliff of this hour and latitude.

Flicker on the fir root, do you find enough to keep you warm?

* * *

Once, I followed the moon around the corner.
West flipped to east. Women dug up coral for necklaces

a thousand miles from the sea. Monkeys
trapezed the cloud-tall rhododendrons.

Fear netted the face of the man beside the trail –
Do you have anything for bleeding? –

the woman behind him in the swept yard
leaking life since the birth two weeks before.

That night the young English trekker sipped smoky tea
and argued *But in my country I am very poor.*

* * *

Flash to way back when. The gossip of early crabs
and sea lice settling in silt. *Psst! Fossils!*

Are you dreaming us? They keep their traps shut
and point too many legs in various directions.

History: story to origami this rising and passing.
End of the end of the year. As if time were served in wedges.

* * *

Obeying the first law of winter (Don't fritter daylight)
you wait till dark to rack the blackberry wine.

The best-seller's face down on the couch, tuckered out
from teaching me how light bends around a black hole,

how space-time has no beginning, and the bits
we're made of are glued by the strongest force.

Not so this sweater I'm knitting for the third time.
Knit ravel, knit ravel. Sleeve of care.

The kids are pleating old calendars into paper birds.
Lakes and endangered mammals flock to the window.

The glass takes positive prints of our doings,
transient fossils, busy busy!

Your vintage is blessed by the goose neck lamp,
metal-hooded monk with a single bright idea.

Tall green bottles hum to a rising pitch.
August has mailed us a postcard.

* * *

This much we do know: how summer presses
molecules from a crowded sky. *(Be leaf. Be juice.)*

How December can clamp the black arteries of water.
Beer came first, and from the sediment the accident

of bread, that other colony of yeast:
Add water, add wheat, presto! it overtops the rims of pans

like last week's time-lapse of snow.
White loaves in the flowerbed sink back to green and grey.

* * *

Cards light on the tabletop and flutter up to another hand.
The children are sorting clubs from spades.

We'll teach them how to end up with nothing.
They laugh and lean back in their chairs.

Clocks and milestones of winter night, and just this
wisp of strategy – heart, a brain, da noive.

What do you want to be when you grow up?
    a. The one that got away.
    b. The one who tells it.

* * *

So this *fish* goes into this *back*eddy.
Maybe it fins its way onto the muddy

air, and the story of legs begins,
but the other fish keep quickening the water.

Picture the new-fashioned tree of life: plants and animals
nothing but twigs in a thicket of bacteria.

Did you know these tiny life-forms, who roll their own DNA,
team up to script each cell in your body?

We are definitely not in Kansas anymore.

* * *

Once, D'Sonoqua pitched camp on these shores,
but not for my people. They introduced themselves,

imported seeds and legends dropping from holes
in their pockets. Foxglove. A half-shell Venus.

She picks her way among the barnacles, muttering *the wine-dark sea.*
Could someone please get her a jacket?

In a universe gone Moebius we end up where we started. Tonight
the black windows offer homespun aliens, dancing a two-dimensional house.

I do not know how much we need to know. Behold
the subatomic particles. How they hug each other so tight.

II

War Baby

One month after Pearl Harbor, the night comes up a norther.
Icy air has wrapped the house like a New Year's gift, spangling every
    sill
My parents are heading to bed.

Listen how the wind, all the way from Inuvik,
ferrets the cracks in the weather stripping,
whispering *what's next?*

Out back the Easter lilies, hunkered underground,
predict the luck that will rise from a victory
garden. They would sign up first thing tomorrow,

pop the question, burn the suicide note.
Crazy hope? Wartime jitters?
My father stubs his cigarette. My mother unpins her hair.

The eaves hold their breath as these two
slip into the pool of tropical light poured by the bedside lamp.
Now

the snowclouds tip their box of blessings –
numberless, individual – onto the fields and houses.
My sister dreams up nickels for a war bond

and I begin
my slow tumble into
rationing and heartbeat and back doors and anchors aweigh.

Aldredge Place

Mirage

What if the only way out
entails heat, a road,
and something that never was
shimmers behind and ahead no matter
how far you travel?

Picture This

Double profile. Girl and doll
ruffled in promise,
a cheque blank as the yard,
the Plymouth, that halo of sky.
Note the buttons down the back,
the sash looped behind. No way
did this princess dress herself.
Long ago in a far land
there were elm trees.
The sidewalk narrows
to the vanishing point.

Listen

Hear the rustle all down the block
as people unwrap the box of the Fifties.
Life will be a clock, a pet,
it will wag its tail and lie

down. Food will glisten in mounds
on the breakfast tables
and skirts will go *taffeta-taffeta*.

The Creek

The children are soldiers of fortune,
pioneers, the whole shooting match.
They are Columbus hunting treasure
in Hemphill Creek, a pavement of fool's gold
so thick they stop collecting.
The creekbed slithers under bridges,
another world where cars whisper
and mothers push sleeping babies
through the pecan shade unaware
of the rattlesnake curled by the water.
The big boys pulp it with rocks
till a father shows up at 5 o'clock
and fetches his shotgun.
The tail will move until sunset somebody says.
This snake fathoms their secrets.
The rattle is a little ear
of corn, a pearly set of baby teeth.

Knowledge will not come
sudden, as in folk tales.
The merchant of knowledge
is a fairy pregnant with dimes
and the price? – all the ivory
they arrived with, one tooth at a time.

The Women. The Heat

The women shimmy
dust-mops out the doors
and stitch little devil suits
for Halloween. They eye the bottles
at the drugstore: *Tabu. My Sin.*

Mrs. Agnew's granddaughter
turns up fat, and tiny shirts join
the Greek blouses and pillowslips
flapping the legendary heat, a dragon
who scorches every corner with his breath.

Mrs. K. lounges bare-breasted
in the backroom of fry-an-egg-on-the-sidewalk
afternoons, lick-thumbing the pages
of *True Romance* until her husband
topples from a train one night
in his robe and slippers.

Mavis just blew in from England
wearing trousers, complaining
there's no place to drink before lunch.

The girl's father laughs
how his headlights bagged Lucy's mother
kissing a man against the elm tree,
the party a yellow square behind them.

Door-To-Door Men

Desert-hungry men march
past the tan brick pillars and sieve
like smoke through the screen doors.
They lay out their offerings:
brushes, tomatoes, sharpened knives.
One leads a pony bearing silver-
studded chaps, a tripod and camera.
The ice-cream man materializes
in a cloud of music
everywhere
at exactly 3:15.
He tugs his leash of song
and little cowgirls and cowboys
ride out with nickels
to ransom what his cold heart hides.

State Hospital

The street piles up against the chain-link
of the State Hospital
(whisper *loony bin*).
Everybody knows somebody who.
Past the wall of airy diamonds
they hoe their corn and potatoes
and look ordinary,
shoes and pockets, ordinary.
Who ate up their trail of bread crumbs?
One-potato two-potato,
anyone could be next
(whisper *shipped away*).
What is straight?
Where is narrow?

Suicide

Lucy's uncle is a movie star,
eyes brooding in sheets of light,
women on their knees
all over town. He visits
and the girl lurks in the crape myrtle
till a shadow passes a window.
Come winter they'll find him
in his New York apartment
and she will overhear the hiss
of a new way to die.

Hair

'I am Rapunzel,' she sings from the porch,
'I live with a witch ...'
Mrs. K. says the girl sings like an angel.
Martha K. pulls the angel into her bedroom
and peels her waistband to show
the first terrible hairs. Mrs. K. yells
Put your shirt on!
and shaves Buddy's head for ringworm.
Buddy refuses to go to school looking like
the French girl in *Life Magazine*
who loved the wrong soldier.

Nuclear Family

Aren't they all? Somewhere a bomb
has a name on it
and her parents lie in bed
Sunday mornings. What if
God's indifference sluices past them too?
She'll suit herself
as a ghost or a devil and shelter
behind the mulberry tree.
She'll chalk squares and number them
to guide the fathers and big sisters
home from the bus.

Glassed-In Porch

Meet the eyes of the man
who stares in the window
and you're good as snatched.
The girl and her brother shuck blankets
on the glassed-in porch and clatter out
to pick leaves for the class silkworms,
carting home measles and chickenpox.
Fevers crack in that box of light,
at night more dark than they can handle.
Charlie from the State Hospital
tucks his demons under his arm
and goes AWOL, navigating the chalk
directions to the bosom of the neighbourhood.
Her brother will swear he spotted him
milky as moonlight beside the garage.

Tortoise

Did I say Columbus, did I say
pioneers? They are hunter-gatherers
stalking the way to grow up.
What they collect is piss-all
plus mulberries to feed their children
and cattle, to dye their homespun
purple. They haul thin bellies
through the privet hedge to meet the tortoise
big as a bike tire and twice as innocent,
meaning he'll have to be stoned too.

The Picture

Who guaranteed this girl horses,
a balcony to let down her hair?
Who gave her a tree that transmutes to silk,
precious metals and safety strong as glass?
I did.
I promised whatever it took
to get her to walk down that sidewalk,
but not yet.
She smiles above the doll's bonnet.
The doll raises her arm,
hailing the sweet ever after like a taxi.

In Juarez

This is the girl's first nightclub, in Juarez.
Kids can get in anywhere in border
towns, the trinketed streets and make-you-sick water.
Wide-hat musicians blare 'La Cucaracha'.
The father buys the girl a Shirley Temple and aims
his gin-soaked toothpick at an olive.

This afternoon they passed alleys alive
with rats and the souvenirs of Juarez,
hands slapping tortillas and hands held out for alms,
the gold cloth, a saint's knuckle stitched in its border
where anyone can kiss it, cockroaches,
bandits, and do the local people drink the water?

Fault of the Pope. That's what her
father says. The band cranks it up for the live
floor show, sequins and shimmying brooches.
The marquee said 'Bestest dancers de Juarez!'
a fraction the price of shows across the border,
and look! – one is the girl's double, there, by the potted palms.

Rhinestones river her look-alike arms.
Her hairdo is the very same ducktail, slicked with water.
Same smile, eyes, colour. (Everyone is brown this side the border.)
If the girl learned Spanish could she live
here? Would she fit right in, in Juarez,
ignoring for the moment the roaches?

She stares and wonders. The music reaches
its climax – maracas, a windmill of arms.
The father, who looks a little like the hero Benito Juarez,
holds his hand up to call the waiter.
The twin's bare back cha-chas toward the rest of her life.
In childish Spanish, the father gives his order.

A dried-up riverbed patrols the border.
Rifles and chainlink, uncountable breaches.
Are there, then, a number of possible lives?
Holes in the expected, like magic charms?
Whisha-whish go the dusty palms. *Answers are water.*
The girl sips the night-sugar taste of Juarez.

Dinner arrives on the arms of the waiter.
The father reaches for his *cabrito*, specialty of Juarez.
Life, whispers the sweating glass at the drink's sweet border.

Halley, 1986

> *Messages from the cosmos arrive addressed*
> *'To whom it may concern.'*
> – Norbert Weiner

What would you make of us tonight,
Daddy? Last pass you were five,
carried out in your nightshirt.
Whenever you told it
we could smell the pipe-smoke
in your father's jacket, see
the neighbours turning their faces
to the blaze across the sky.
A body could read a newspaper
by its light, and the omens –
better times coming, or worse.
You always said *I won't be around for the next one*,
but we could do the arithmetic, lots of men
make it that far.

For us the future was everywhere,
we swam in it. Cars with fins
drifted by, and those life preservers you tossed –
we boogied right past them, you yelling
Turn that thing down! while we rocked
around the clock. We grabbed our own tiny life-
rings, a flavour for every colour,
and held them on our tongues, secrets
dissolving to splinters.

Little news this time, a pale smudge
no one would notice, and you long since KO'ed
by the fist of your heart.
Lucky the sky has cleared at the dark
of the moon and what we're looking for
is close to something we can find.
We have to try, raised as we were
on the slow suck of expectation.
Would you think there'd be augury
as well in this failure to astonish?

Early Years: Her Kitchen

Plop, splish, into the saucepan.
My mother stands at the counter, spooning
spinach out of a can.
Through the window drift
the grannies she was named for,
gauzy as Woolworth curtains.
Are they shocked at the expense,
the laziness? Amazed at such convenience?
My mother doesn't give two hoots.
She won't be serving soupy histories
from the stewpot. Not even the one
where her grandfather bought it
that day on the ranch, penned
in the pasture by the crazy bull.
She's moved on. Fetched up
in this field of black and white
squares that hopscotch from the hall
to the oven to the wap-wap
of the screen door.
Hoping it's far enough.

Later Years: Her Mornings

Downstairs, the woman who has left
her own children's hungers two busrides away
is dusting a white woman's bookshelves.
If this is one of the venues where
Billie and Bessie got the blues,
the lyric segues into the sad, hollow cello
of a woman with not enough to do.
My mother sits in the chintz-covered
wing chair, hazed in filter-tip.
She has girded herself in pink elastic.
Nylons, a slip and a housecoat, ready,
should the morning or inclination mutter,
to lift her arms toward a dress
and sally forth. Appearances are what
she will keep up until she gives up
making them. Her children will catalogue
blanks of attention,
a failure to focus beyond
the scrim of tobacco. She taps her blood-
coloured nails. The chair offers grace,
for a time, the lap of a stub-winged angel.

Altar

Worship, we'd have called it –
if we'd thought that way. Our father
put it like this: There's one
who holds the hand and one
who kisses it. Which didn't
make much sense until it dawned
he meant *holds out*. We pictured them
beyond the door, him on his knees,
maybe, our mother's arm
extended. Anyone could see
who depended.
                    But that morning
he crashed to the tiles clutching
the bottle of heart pills, it
cut her loose. The next twenty years
she drifted, a boat
with no mooring.
                    For my brother
this proves we had it wrong:
whose hand, whose lips.
I say all that worship anchored her.
Take away the supplicant
and the altar's nothing but a table.
Dust gathers, mice move in.
Mecca? – just another wide spot,
the Ganges only a river
where women beat the daylights
out of cloth and arrange it
over the rocks to dry.

Closet Suicide

They won't let you stay in your condo
after your grandson, *vroom*ing his dump truck
among the high heels on your closet floor,
comes across the pistol.

A thing like that does put you at the mercy of your children.

They will arrive, close their eyes,
rest their foreheads on their hands for a minute
and suck in a breath. The breath will taste the crack in the earth
running the length of the room, the one too many
drink-invited comas. It will whisper
we can't let you live like this anymore.

They will find a Home, where none-of-their-damned-business
is boiled up for lunch. Where in spite of the nurses'
baby-talk, in spite of the far-goners
parked in wheelchairs up on Three,
choices remain.

You can become a guerrilla, go underground,
take out one piece at a time.
Fall. Break your arm. Refuse
the stretches and lifts the bright young thing from Physio brings.
That smoke-choked bone is hungry for oxygen?
a bouquet of vitamins? Be firm. The arm will
heal funny, you won't have to reach for anything
again. This works for ankles too. Funny bones.

Keep still. You'll get smaller, a daily departure.
Forget snow's blessing, and jonquils,
the relief of a shaded verandah.
Be the very autumn, constantly leaving.
Shrink to three sharp grains, oystered in the hearts
of your children, who were sure they were worth
sticking around for. Weren't they.

My Father Drops By

He's always dropping by like this.
Out of the blue he'll whisper *Thrift, thrift,* as I marry
the sliver to the fresh bar of soap.
He stands by the lettuce patch, I say *Look –
ripe tomatoes!* I spill the beans, a one-woman Fall Fair.

So it's no surprise when he genies up from the box of letters
I stumble across in the attic, the jumble I sort
to make room for the squash and the garlic.

That father was my age exactly when he scribbled
I miss you so much to the girl who'd just gone off to college,
who thought he wrote clichés. He was surfacing
from a heart attack that walloped him good,
six weeks flat on his back. He missed my graduation
to let the famous cardiac centre crank his ribs back
and open his heart – one of the first, the orderly
shaving his chest said *Gee, ain't ya scared?*

Five good years to keep on smoking and drinking.
They hadn't invented cholesterol yet, or Type A.
I was seventeen. Hadn't a clue how parent-love
rents one of the heart's red rooms and never moves out.
I didn't recognize a chain letter or know I'd be bound to send it on.

III

Not the Whole Story

The theatre's gone, the laundromat,
even the A&P where I'd heap brown bags
at the baby's feet, the prince
of groceries, one load so heavy it broke
an axle and I navigated the frost-heaved
bricks on two wheels. 1967, Summer
of Love, whatever had flowered for us
the year before had leaked through cracks
in the plaster, quicksilver
down the sloped floorboards,
draining out parted seams built to an earlier
code – a wooden fire escape, of all things.

How to tease out the fairy tale
mornings, me and the baby and the ticking
antique clock. We rocked in the yellow chair,
motes hanging in pale columns
that slanted through rippled glass.
We filled the watery light
and harboured no memories.

Here's where I unlocked the carriage
from the wrought iron railing.
Off duty cabbies shouted from the tavern,
Let us see the baby,
let us look after him! – and what
was I to say? – one nocturnal creature
to another. One midnight I knelt

at the streetlit window, tiny mouth
to my breast, watching the closing-hour
screams and punches, woman drunk, man
drunk. Such passion a foreign country,
rage to the point of claws.

That first week home with the baby,
my husband's anger at my friends
mopping and baking – who could fathom
this need for privacy? Now I see
he was a porcupine inside out, any touch
might spike another tender place.
No wonder I couldn't find him – my repeated
inaudible shrieks, my echolocation.
I'd signed a poisonous deal but decided
to stick to it and besides
I knew my way out was bone dry
and waiting for a spark.

Time Travel

Beside me my son, child again
in his little boots and life jacket.
I steer the dream boat parallel

to shore, cliffs I've never noticed.
Who's the old woman dropping her line
across the gunwale as if there were salmon?

The wind picks up and I bail
with the square tobacco can.
Waves are swamping the boat

and I've grown no gills. The bottom
lies distant as the chance to do it over.
In sci-fi movies they spot the ringer

from the future. Something foils the plan
and history happens. The shocking fact,
when the Inuit met us, was that we hit

our children. If this dream were night
there'd be phosphorescence, a necklace
of stars. Raising a child is a one-way trip

but no one told me this till later.
Surely these parkas will float us both ashore.
I stitched them with my own teeth and fingers.

Nonsense

Cleaning fish is a tidy phrase
for slipping a knife-point into the anus
and sawing in tiny strokes
to the bone harness behind the gills.
For sliding your fingers into the slit,
easing the heart guts liver
free from their membrane and scraping
the upright knife-blade against the lay
of the scales, a broadcast of silver-chips.

Cleaning fish is what I was doing
the afternoon of my husband's third heart attack.
That and singing silly songs a mile and a half
from the phone line, no way to hear
him gasping for air in the city. *Mairzy doats*
we shouted, the children bent in laughter
at such nonsense.

We were sure this was how he would go,
high-strung and no one could see
what was eating him.
Three little fishes inna itty bitty pool.
One of the boys leafed a comic,
Biff! Bam! you're down, your eyes turn to x's.
The neighbour who had a telephone
filled the doorway and opened his mouth.
Swim said the mama fish swim if you can
but we were drowning in air, nothing
made sense, my knife
shooting wet stars all over the cabin.

1970s: Domestic

Here is the table, scattershot with cake crumbs, candles like soldiers on a cold ground. Jam jars cup lakebeds of red wine. On the floor, the children in pint-size sleeping bags. This is the night no one remembers the chickens, the coop over where the new house looks finished but isn't, come morning four hens and the rooster dazed in a corner, twenty corpses around the yard, one mink-bite to each neck. And this is us

hammer and saw, hellbent on escaping another winter in that leaky shack. No time for it, or the heart, so a neighbour stacks the flame-feathered bodies in his truck and drives them home to can. I rinse off last night's candles to celebrate a dozen times more. Domestic economy.

The shack will grow up to be a tool shed and later the younger boy's proof that he can move out too. My husband will thin and thin in the upstairs bedroom, past walking, past hope, past his birthday, needing some things I can supply, some I can't.

Javelinas

Three people in a car headed south
toward the border.
The one who lives here
tells the two whose car it is
they'll see javelinas
if they come the back way.
They come to what passes for woods
in these parts, and the gas cap
finally slides off the roof.
Back ways are his specialty,
he's officially going bankrupt
while contriving to keep his money,
stashing the best things
at his mother-in-law's house
and scrounging substitutes.
'Tiled table' the inventory says.
Last night they sat up smoking
a great deal, glueing shards
from various bathroom jobs
onto a Goodwill bench circa 1953.

This is the guy who will drop by
the treatment centre hotel
four years down the road
to stare at the ceiling and hold forth
about his latest field trip to Pakistan.
How his wife traipsed off with the nomads.
Never once will he ask after
his old friend's condition
(pain) or prospects (nil).

They will wish this guy would try
to connect, but then they don't
either, the man under morphine,
the woman fogged in disbelief.
That night her dreams will keep
trotting into an ugly wood
and something that could blow up any minute
will drift the dry air.

Negative Space, 1980

Everyone said I was holding up.
What else to do? Ten school lunches a week,
tomatoes turning, dahlias to lever
out of the cold and wet.

But there were times.
Unexpected tears above the breadknife.
Some nights driving a back road I'd have to pull over
and wait for it to pass.

I gave the wheelchair to the Red Cross. Distributed trinkets,
finally found someone long-armed enough for the sweater.
I barely knew him and never saw him again
but he liked the Lifesaver stripes, my bold period.

Each day the tide slipped out and I walked on the bottom of the sea
I started to say *absence* but it wasn't that.
More like noticing the shapes cast by the edges
of things. Cup and spoon, rock and willow.

Learning how that space can vanish in other ways
than objects moving close.
That space between us we'd filled or emptied
like a woodshed, and winter on its way.

IV

Islands

Food, shelter, clothing, boat.
Three-quarters of the earth is water.

1860, Tucker Bay

A shipload of lice and men enters
the bay. The captain, itching
to leave a mark, christens the waters

for his friend, another captain
out somewhere naming things. A dice
of islands channels the current and the wind.

The two tallest put him in mind
of his friend's boys, who laughed
by the fireplace

the last time he was home.
Back in England,
Jervis and Jedediah Tucker,

chasing a puppy through a tide
of bluebells, stop.
Each stands suddenly alone,

shoved up from some hot place
and frozen in air. The puppy barks
at their gravelled feet. A certainty

settles over them:
the balance of their lives will be mapped
in salt.

A Floating Island

threads the bay at sunset, passengers
against the railings. Imagine –
a completely white ship, lights enough

to shock a northern town in December.
Everyone expects something:
shuffleboard, liar's dice, one kiss

at least, before the gangplank.
Sleeping in slots
below the waterline, down three flights

and everything bolted in place.
Sliced meats glisten on porcelain platters,
steaming toward glaciers.

Do we think we'll find love wearing party clothes?
Ice sculpture and too much wine
and still this hunger.

Local Phenomena

The far island lifts mirages
along its beach like petticoats, each boat,
every summer house buoyed in water

above the waterline.
A friend saw a cube of highrises upside down
off a wooded point. Thought she was losing it.

How does it feel – the tug captain,
the cottagers – to dance on air?
You can bring these chunks of light

closer with binoculars, and they photograph
well – who's to say what's real? –
though like subatomic particles and love

they vanish if you get too close.

If You Lived Here You'd Be Home Now

(Nepal, 1996)

Hard to find anyplace
that's not a theme park.
The path from temple to temple,

the red-dot third eye. Attention
birdwatchers! Over four hundred species!
How about an ascent to the world's roof,

bright-suited mammals reaching for hand-holds?
If we go there will we find the red dot,
the arrow, the You-Are-Here?

Will the five-dollar guru say his karma
just ran over our dogma?
Altitude sickness shows the narrow slot

we're fit for. *Descend!*
shout the guidebooks, the only medicine.
There are local names for these ice-fields,

and seashells wink from the rocks
at twelve thousand feet. Back home we'll fasten
little squares of proof in an album:

Here is where we went, and *here*.

Night Island

> *Once you have slept on an island*
> *You'll never be quite the same!*
> — R.L. Field

You can't be too careful where your dreams go.
Here they escape woolen covers
to shinny past the roofbeam and drift

among hemlocks. The bright-hot bakery
pulses to all-night radio, the beat
of dough on a floured board.

Maps here call for a pinch of salt,
but the heart wanders where it will,
never mind the homespun wisdom

reeling from almanac pages to lie
in snaky piles on the linoleum hissing
This way! This way!

Maybe your mother told you
Always mix your cakes in a yellow bowl.
Your dreams remember swimming

in phosphorescence – mermaids, galaxies.
They worm themselves into spirals
of cinnamon stacked on checkered napkins.

Home at dawn, the baker doesn't see
the night picked over. Taken away
in paper bags or eaten right there

with gossip and coffee.

The Heart

> *Islands are metaphors for the heart,*
> *no matter what poet says otherwise.*
> — Jeanette Winterson

We lug two-by-tens, a claw-foot bathtub,
sacks of lime off the ferry. Islands,
they say, are critical stop-offs for trade

and migration, but I say
whatever comes to an island stays.
That the dark-feathered griefs

and crates of desire calling at any heart
will dock and take up residence.
The heart hauls its reasons like a low-budget

traveller, everything crammed in one backpack,
impossible to set down a single souvenir
without walking away from it all.

How surprised we were in Greece at the packs
leaning against the monument gates,
their owners trudging the pale hills.

If only I could live like that: know
that all the love and sorrow I ever needed
is there. Here.

V

A Brief History of Time

Each day we walk through the famous graveyard.
Oak, viburnum and sweet-gum
have dropped their fruit to the ground.
Pillars and downcast angels cluster around us
as we stuff our pockets with seeds.
We came to Boston by train,
the tight room, where each thing collapsed
into something else, and the view was rivers and flatlands.
All through the trip I've carried the difficult book.
Time, it seems, has a history.
The universe lacks edges but swarms with tiny dimensions.
The pull between us is fine as the old days.
It is autumn. Trees have abandoned chlorophyll
for what they've been hiding all along.
In Imaginary Time the clock runs either direction.
You could die before you were born.
A cup might gather its pieces and fly back up to the table.
This is one dream.
The author doesn't touch the thornier mysteries
such as how two bodies cleave,
meaning both cling and separate.
Our bags are a stash of little torn-paper packets
to smuggle home behind the puzzle
of how to make love go the distance.
Cut-leaf beech, the ginkgo's nervous fans –
this dream of a hardwood forest.

Field Report

(for Sam, 4 lbs. 9 oz.)

You're here at last.
They tell me you look like a tiny old man –
Merlin, coming at it backwards.
The Mayans say we face the past.
That the future sails at our backs, towing.
Once, I made it almost to Maya country
but turned back north toward the Aztecs.
All I know is this: wherever I went
people offered me bread or opened a door.
Soon you'll walk out among the ten thousand things.
Logical rooms will whisper *If this, then that,*
but Sammy, remember the bread and the doorways.
Today I watched a raven fly back to its nestlings,
the new-hatched robin a heavy rag in its beak.
You'll be asking how long this light, how big is air.
What can I promise? That everything must eat.

Oaxaca: Renoir's 'Luncheon of the Boating Party'

I know I'm expected to bargain,
to argue the fractions of pennies,
but how do I find the words
among pyramids of carrot and mango?
Women in black whisper *Mira los ojos,*
my sons' pale eyes. What they're admiring
is absence, but haven't dreams
always trafficked in hunger?

Nights here stay hot as geckoes
on rent-by-the-week walls. I slip
into a dream of the painted crowd
scene, its frame a tropic
I can step across to the linseed air.
Look how much wine they've put away! –
nothing left but a squeeze of red paint.
Imagine the loaves that scattered
such crusts on the table. The awning
flutters its heart murmur, tossing

a net of gazes: She watches him
but he's looking at the other one
who stares at the man in front and he
can't take his eyes off the woman
smooching the dog. What they wouldn't give
to look somewhere, anywhere, else!
Across the river, say, into a book.
Whatever the people in famous paintings
get to do. And what language
do they think in? How would you say
I'd do anything to get you
to turn and look at me.

Instructions to the Rain

Five nights too late
they find her friend in his boat.
It's rained all week, ta-*tock*
ta-*tock* on the porch.
Whatever was left unsaid
will stay that way.
The rain stops eavesdropping
as the geese coast in
a-*honk* a-*honk*.
Did you know that cry
is the two of them? Call and
response, iambic for life,
the beat her friend knew by heart
and then, with no excuses, forgot.
Too late to remind him to
come again some other day.

December 6th

(Fifth anniversary of the Montreal massacre)

Into the morning drizzle and snowpatch
to see the year's second-highest tide.
No. To witness it.
Familiar weeds and beaches plunged
into unaccustomed salt. A gun-metal

sky. Along the shore
we make sure the boats are tied.
(An escaping boat always holds a good story.
The Boston Whaler upside down
off Lund, the officer who phoned

afraid he was notifying the bereaved.)
We come to the logs we spiked and roped
last summer, ganged at the back of the bay.
If logs could talk: the seed, the coming-of-age,
the time in water. They float, speechless,

stories that will shuttle into ours:
fenceposts around the new field, roof-shakes,
wide boards to sheath a building.
For now they wait, good children
in a classroom. Lay your heads on your desks.

I'll tell you fourteen stories.
Fifteen. There was no rescue.
No escape. The numbers
on the tide chart and calendar summon us:
Witness.

Crossing

Coming home, January:
slate-dark waves
are an argument of mountains
that lift and erode,
flashback to some liquid beginning of time.
The ferry plunges and climbs.

For balance I keep my eyes on the harbour
we've just left.
Its marker is a white stroke
in a grey-on-grey wash,
smaller and smaller,
a vanishing toy.

Finally, nothing but rain-furred
land humps and the seven-foot ghosts
of spray our wake makes.

This
is what we do to live
where we live.

These waters have taken
several people I know. Knew.
Small boats, weather, margins
most on this crossing have tested.

Perspective shifts. One island
slips behind another.

No matter I'm standing under shelter,
I back into the afternoon with salt
on my face, hanging on to what's
close by and hard.

Chaos, February 2nd

If a butterfly's flap can jitterbug everything.
If nobody knows where the snows went,
never mind whether they'll come. If
what's been memorized was a left-behind
language anyway: *Whan that Aprille,
Où sont les neiges* –
how do we handle this day
clobbered by a record low,
day set aside for a shadow or its absence?
Goldfinches in olive drab
drop like mercury to the iced-up sidewalk.
Students leaving the sheltered workshop
wave bye-bye from the bus
whose number they've got.
The woman in the Queen Elizabeth hat
mutters *half pint low*
but we're all slow learners
at this bus stop, here at the edge
of the range map, expecting
a Back East groundhog to cast
anything we could use.
Come April these birds will gild
the treble clef of the fence
with yester-*year!*, yester-*year!*
Till then it's peck and scritch
on holiday pay. Pipes crack
all across town as they study
the alchemy of feathers into gold.

Cousins

She's so open, we'd say, *she never holds back.*
We'd come away shaking our heads, what more
could her body do to her, the body as carnivore,
a Venus flytrap, it would get her yet. Carol was open,
a carillon, bellflower, the dozen delicate throats
tolling all that blue perfume onto the baked afternoon,
onto the bees with their stingers, their needles
knives and i.v. ports, finally the port for the feeding tube, oh
she was open, what more could the doctors do,
they've only got two hands you know,
subtracting a problem with the left hand,
bringing one on with the right. *Stay out of the sun,*
no we mean really stay out of it, this was ages
before everybody ducked behind sleeves and hats,
here are the snapshots, this was the family reunion
we roasted ourselves on the beach,
oiled and revolving, grandmothers, babies,
Carol must be off somewhere in the shade.

Five years on at the lake cottage, it was who
could suck the last drop of ambrosia out of a lobster claw.
Carol's problem was how to feed half a stomach.
Then how to feed at all. The last time I saw her,
my sister and I forked up artichoke hearts while Carol
nibbled a sliver of off-limits Brie and cracked
jokes about paying later. Now I get it.
We'll each take a turn at being the oldest cousin.

Elegy

(for Terry Hernandez)

Days begun in song-sparrow set in the varied
thrush, hope to blue
if I ever heard it. April, April,
potatoes boxed
in the barn wake up and imagine
multitudes, and
that's the sugar and the sting, isn't it –
that things go on.
Tonight a lemonpeel moon gets snagged in the willow's bare
branches. One star
studs the moon's dark edge and I think
Wait a minute,
don't we drag the moon behind us like a stubborn
pup? I wait a
minute. The star blips out just as the season's first bat
flip-flutters by.
The bat brailles the universe with
little fingers
of sound spelling angle! crevice!
wall, and then wall.

The Last Bright Morning

This is the last bright morning
before the high pass we won't cross,
the slopes rolling up raggedy cuffs of snow.
Soon we'll turn for the trek down
through the same rivers and villages
though nothing's truly the same from the North.
Sadhus walk this route, all bare
feet and begging bowl, their drape
of orange and saffron, some of them stoned,
and we are stoned, on rice, on altitude,
on stones, *namasté, namasté*, to each
descending traveller. Our heads hurt,
our lungs pant like puppies
but we push on, past the vat of barley
fermenting in the sun, past the couple
hauling the plow and seedbasket to the rock-
stunned field, through the gauntlet of trailside
weavers and cafés pouring pricey sodas,
to the tiny old woman who for a nickel
will spin the giant prayer wheel and let you snap
her photo, on up to the flame that burns on water.
Here are the poplars sprouted from Lord Krishna's
footsteps. Did he clap his hands, and laugh,
at the whole tall burden of air suddenly missing?

You Take Me to Your Hometown

You never said the shortcut was ten tracks wide.
It zigzags the daylight between the wheels
of the stopped cars. No way out for the kid
caught under there that day you stayed home.
Your parents shipped themselves to this wrong-side
kitchen window where your mother,
hand to mouth, waited for the ka-
blang of coupling trains.
If she looked again, would England be out there?

Squint and there's my own Main Street, *Bambi*
at the Bijoux, blindsided by the dust it was headed for.
Saskatchewan, Texas, the glass bricks of Gem Cafés
everywhere made passersby go blobby. Farmers
and businessmen bowed their hats over coffee
and children turned to angels in the snow.

We itched into coats or shucked shoes for whatever
winter or summer hustled our way.
Tonight we'll hire a room where our hands
can travel to places we only dreamed of
back then. Numbered streets chased the compass
into wheatfields, cottonfields, and would not meet
even at infinity. Is this how we recognized each other?
Arriving like dark-eyed revelations
backlit by all that space, by the passion
those seasons picked up over the prairie.

San Josef Bay

When I mention how long it took to get here
I don't mean that day we kept pulling over
to let the rain let up. What I mean is
the years before even unfolding the map.
Each route to saltwater beckoned
but you kept answering *next time.*

We've pitched our tent on a plate edge
that's tilting beneath the mainland.
Someone has set three foil-wrapped candies
beside the sign about bears.
I sit under a rigged-up tarp to sketch
the unsketchable:
seafoam hissing in and out,
mist-ghosts over the rivermouth.

Other ghosts, too: early settlers
living on the government's hollow
promise of a road. Before them, the first
people, hanging around for the guaranteed
break in the weather. And us?
Like the squirrel stashing another cone
as the raven croaks *Oh yeah?*
we can't help stuffing ourselves with hope.
We stew it up on a little campstove,
slip into blue ripstop cocoons,
flight, iridescence, camouflage.

Rain Starts and Stops

Rain starts and stops
and starts, unpredictable
as the old blue truck.
It grinds my gears till my door
falls off. A thousand quick-
silver tears hit the deck but where
can they go? Exactly where they want,

Heron Bay, Strait of Georgia, Western
Hemisphere, this cold tenth of August.
You walk through the room,
notice what I'm reading and ask
if *Getting the Love You Want*
is the sequel to *Wanting the Love
You Get*. The garden takes off its shirt

and cloud songs smash the larger flowers.
Dahlias and gladiolas fall down laughing
at ol' Susie imagining she could lash them to sticks
like martyrs. La belle dame sans merci. No thanks.
Ticka-ticka, the sewing machine needle
lifts and pokes like a Short-billed dowitcher
at low tide. Who can fathom the rick-rack

of love? It once looked easy as solving
the numbers for pi. The forsythia whispers
'I thought I'd heard it all till I listened
to nothing.' You come in the other door
just as the radio tells us the monarchs
are back in power. *Good!* you say. *I like it
when the butterflies are in charge.*

Nomad

One time we paddled deep
into the sound where northern
and southern tides meet,
the water so warm
oysters spawn. Such relief
from the world's coming and going.
Whenever we pulled ashore
you hauled out the matches
and kettle. I scavenged
twigs for the fire. It was clear
why I'd picked you.
I saw the essence of *nomad*.
Not the moving, anyone
can do that. It's the knowing
that no matter where we stop
we've brought everything we need.

Acknowledgements

I am grateful to the many people whose intelligence, keen eyes and ears, honesty, encouragement, and good humour have helped to shape these poems. In particular I would like to thank Don McKay, Jan Zwicky, Erin Mouré, Patricia Young, Gary Draper, the Nanaimo Women Poets Group, the Lasqueti Island Writers Group, and the Banff Centre. Warm thanks to my family and friends and community, and especially to Peter Johnston.

This book is for Peter.

Some of the poems in this book have been previously published in *The Malahat Review, Poetry Canada, Event, The Fiddlehead, The Texas Observer, Willow Springs, Arc, Grain, The Antigonish Review, Quarry*, the chapbook *Islands* (Reference West, 1996) and the League of Canadian Poets anthology, *Vintage 95*.

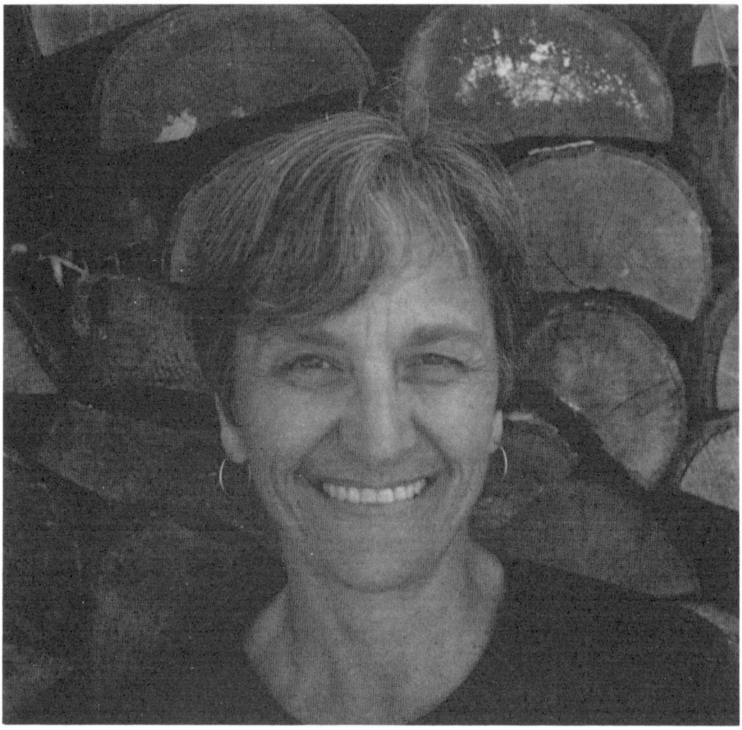

Sue Wheeler grew up in Texas and now lives on a seaside farm on Lasqueti Island, B.C. Her first book, *Solstice on the Anacortes Ferry*, won the Kalamalka New Writers Prize and was shortlisted for both the Pat Lowther and the Gerald Lampert memorial awards. This is her second collection.